How to Delegate Effectively Without Losing Control

To Drew.

Best of luck.

Pete

How to
Delegate
Effectively
without
Losing
Control

by

Peter A. Land
MS, CSP, CMC, CPCM

Copyright © 2006 by Peter A. Land
Library of Congress Number: 2005903461
ISBN-10: 1-60013-175-1
ISBN-13: 978-1-60013-175-2

Over the past 50 years, I have collected pithy one-liners, quotes, and bits of wisdom about leadership and management. Some I have created, some I have heard or read, others have been shared with me by workshop participants on four continents. I share a sample of them in this book for your enjoyment, and hopefully, enlightenment. I take no credit, even for those I have created. If anyone can provide the original source of any of these quotes, I will gladly give appropriate credit in subsequent editions of this book.

This book was printed in the United States of America.

dedication

The process of writing a book is rarely accomplished alone; there are always skilled colleagues who help shape, refine, and improve the manuscript. I dedicate this book to Chapman Greer, MLS, MA, Ph.D, who has been a major contributor to not only this work but also my first two books.

She has been honored for her work as a college English professor because she has mastered the language. Chapman was a relentless advocate for you, the reader. For her skills, insight, perspective, and encouragement, I will be forever grateful.

contents

preface

Managers at all levels can benefit from learning to delegate. Effective delegation is a key developmental strategy that helps them train, motivate and coach their teams. This is a book about delegation – why it's important and how to do it successfully.

Most people get promoted to management because they're good at their original jobs. The best salespeople become sales managers; the best accountants become accounting managers . . . and so it goes.

However, the very skills and talents that earned them their promotions can bear the seeds of trouble in the management arena. Their self-esteem and the respect they earned from others were based on skills related to their former jobs. Now, they're evaluated on a whole new set of criteria: how well they train, develop, motivate, and coach salespeople and accountants.

Uncomfortable in these new roles, the managers often resort to doing what feeds their feelings of self-worth and earns continued respect from others. They continue doing their old jobs and neglect their more important new leadership responsibilities.

By learning to delegate effectively, such managers can demonstrate true leadership by using their own technical expertise to develop their subordinates.

Delegation is only successful when a manager meets four key criteria in delegating a task to an employee:

1. The employee must have the appropriate skills.

2. The employee must be motivated or willing.

3. The employee must have the necessary resources (tools, equipment, time, money, personnel, etc.)

4. The employee must have the guidance of a timely feedback system to ensure performance meets or exceeds standards. If not, the manager must be prepared to take corrective action, which will have been planned in advance.

How to Delegate Effectively without Losing Control teaches a fail-safe process for satisfying all four critical requirements. This sensible method will free up more time for managers to handle high-impact issues and give subordinates opportunities to grow and learn—a win-win result for everyone.

acknowledgments

Writing a book is such a personally engrossing experience that it is easy to lose sight of one major premise—this book is written for you, not me. I have asked several talented colleagues to proofread and critique this book on your behalf. They did an honest and devoted job of representing you—the reader and ultimate beneficiary of this book.

Once again I turned to a few colleagues whose insights helped improve my first two books, *Managing to Get the Job Done* and *How to Build a Winning Team (And Have Fun Doing It!)*: Margaret Carpenter, former Business Person of the Year in Alabama; Gail Kelley-Webb, President of St. Charles Consulting in Luling, Louisiana; Roger E. Herman, CSP, CMC, President, The Herman Group, Greensboro, North Carolina; Lenny Schaefer; Bill Land, retired business executive; and Beth Cookston all shared their unique perspectives to help make this book even more valuable to you. I owe my heartfelt appreciation to Melanie LeMay for her extraordinary editorial skills and advice.

Much of my success as a consultant and trainer has been greatly influenced by the superb research of my respected friend, Richard W. Leatherman, Ph.D., SPHR.

introduction

Several years ago I received a phone call from the CEO of a large engineering company asking me to work with Joe, one of his most loyal vice presidents. When I asked what the CEO had in mind, he said he was afraid the company was going to lose Joe. I asked if that were a result of retirement, resignation, or illness, and I was told that Joe was working himself to death. I agreed to come and talk with Joe.

A few days later, I walked into Joe's office at 9:00 a.m. His office was a disaster. I had to move a stack of papers from a chair to sit down. He had not seen the top of his desk in months. It was completely covered in documents, files, blueprints, financial statements, letters—you get the picture.

Joe's desk was a representation of his life. Twenty-five pounds overweight, his seventh cigarette of the day seemed like a really bad idea. Working 60 to 70 hours a week had forced him into marriage counseling in an effort to save a 30-year marriage. His 19-year-old son shared little more than the same address with Joe. And Joe's work relationships were not much better than his personal ones. His staff wasn't growing, and he had a high turnover rate.

Joe had started with the company immediately after graduating from high school. The company had paid most of his night school tuition. He completed an undergraduate engineering degree over a seven-year period. He had excelled in every job he had been assigned, and he had been promoted regularly. The company had paid for Joe's graduate degree and even allowed him to leave work early three days a week, with full pay, to attend classes, until he received his master's degree. As a result of his education, training, and work ethic, Joe had accomplished more than his middle-class parents, and his salary exceeded the salaries of his two older brothers—combined!

Joe told me his primary loyalty was to his company. "I owe this company everything," he said. "They paid for two college degrees. I feel my department should do the absolute best job possible for the company and the customer. While I've got good people, they don't have my experience. I don't mean to brag, but the truth is, I can do things better myself. I just can't let the company down. I know I work long hours and take work home at night and on weekends, but I feel great loyalty to the company. My wife and son appreciate our lovely home in a great neighborhood, but I don't think they fully appreciate what it takes to really succeed in business."

Later that day I met with the CEO, who said, "When I ask Joe to take time off, he becomes so appreciative of my concern that he works even harder. He's too young for early retirement. I can't fire him, but I'm afraid he will die at his desk!"

During the next two days of one-on-one executive coaching, Joe and I worked on time management, planning, priority setting, and organizational skills, but the bulk of our activity was to teach Joe *how to delegate effectively without losing control.* I left Joe with the tools necessary to effect sweeping life changes, and his situation motivated him to apply those tools.

Six months later, Joe called me at home. He told me that he was working 35 to 40 hours per week and rarely took work home. His staff had never been happier or more productive. He had joined a health club and was meeting with a personal trainer three times a week. His physician had given him a complete physical and put him on a reasonable diet.

Joe had quit smoking. He'd lost 20 pounds and never felt better. He even had to buy new clothes. He and his son had played in the father-son golf tournament and although Joe had played poorly, they'd had a great time together. Joe and his wife had just returned from a second honeymoon in Bermuda and even had a better sex life!

Joe said, "I just wanted you to know that those delegation skills you made me learn and practice have not only saved my health, my marriage, my relationship with my son, and my job—but in truth they have saved my life!"

This book will teach you what Joe learned.

"

An average solution delivered on time is better than a good solution that's late.

The easiest way to compliment someone is to listen to him or her.

Delegation is an investment in the future health of your organization.

"

"

Delegation gives your organization "bench strength."

Listeners are popular everywhere in the world.

"The best executive is the one who has sense enough to pick good people to do what he wants done, and self-restraint enough to keep from meddling with them while they do it.

Theodore Roosevelt

"

chapter ONE
The Basics

The number-one pressure on managers today is *time*; we never seem to have enough time. The average executive works 14 to 16 hours per day to accomplish all the tasks required of a successful executive, which is a staggering stress load for anyone to shoulder. Research reveals that in the next twelve months, more than 250,000 managers in America below age 65 will *die* as a result of unmanaged stress.

From this book you will learn that delegating effectively, without losing control, is a great stress reliever. In fact, delegation is an executive survival skill, a crown jewel for successful task execution. This book will examine that jewel carefully before putting it in your pocket.

During our journey together, we will ground ourselves in the terms and concepts of delegation, and we will study the many benefits that flow to people who delegate. There are also many benefits for the person to whom tasks are being delegated, or "the delegatee," and, of course, benefits that flow to the organization and the customer. When the aforementioned people win, success is almost guaranteed. The ultimate benefactors are all the stakeholders associated with the enterprise.

There are many barriers, both real and imagined, that operate to inhibit, discourage, and stifle delegation. We will confront these barriers in order to destroy them. We will learn what tasks are reasonable for delegation. We will help you select the best delegatee, and finally, we will master the techniques that ensure success.

Terms and Concepts

As an international management consultant for more than 25 years, I have asked thousands of managers worldwide, "What is a manager's job?" The responses are varied, but most include "to direct people toward a common goal," "to use resources wisely," or "to make a profit." All are true, and all are incomplete. Here is a better definition of a manager's job:

To direct the resources and efforts of the organization toward the efficient accomplishment of the mission or the firm's goals while contributing to the professional development of its personnel.[1] In my workshops I add the tagline *"and have fun doing it!"*

The first portion of this definition, "to direct the resources of the organization to the efficient accomplishment of the mission or the firm's goals," tends to be objective (metrics-oriented) and relatively short-term (monthly or quarterly), which means the manager will be credited for success and blamed for failure. This viewpoint reflects the position that results are generally easy to measure in the short term.

In contrast, the final portion of the definition, "while contributing to the professional development of its personnel and have fun doing it," is very subjective (feelings-oriented), long-term (yearly or longer), and difficult to measure.

When I present this complete definition to participants in workshops, I often experience a loud silence. The group realizes that they have focused most of their energy and effort on the objective, short-term aspects of their job and, in turn, paid pitifully little attention to the long-term, developmental objectives all managers share. Delegation, as a developmental strategy, weighs more heavily in the second part of the definition. For example, as a manager, you are going to demonstrate one of the 27 discrete skills managers perform, namely decision making, coaching, solving problems, resolving conflicts, assigning tasks, etc.

One day one of your subordinates will notice and be impressed with your results. He will file his observation in his memory bank for future reference.

Five years later, that subordinate will encounter a similar problem or challenge and need that skill. That pressure will cause him to recall the way you handled such a problem five years previously. He will do just as you did, and your solution will probably work equally well for him. You will be there, contributing to his success and development, but—I am sorry to say—you will probably not get the credit for that support. Bottom line: The development facet of a manager's job is subjective, difficult to measure, and you often get no credit for your efforts.

The tagline, "and have fun doing it," is not frivolous. I am completely serious that a manager's job must be fun. It has been my experience that managers who push products out the door (objective) while developing their people (subjective) invariably have fun. Problems and stress occur when managers only perform the first half of their job. Some managers incorrectly feel they have no developmental responsibility: "My job is to push products out the door. It is Human Resources' job to develop our people, not mine." Or,

"People should take charge of their own development . . . the cream will rise . . . the talent will claw its way to the top." These managers create a climate of competition, conflict, and stress. And nobody has any fun in such a workplace.

Truly successful managers accept and internalize both the objective and subjective aspects of their profession. They push more and better products out the door because their people are well-trained, highly motivated, have all the tools and resources they need, and are in a constant stage of growth and development. In a word, they make money, "wow" the customer, and have a hell of a lot of fun in the process.

The countless managers I have consulted with over the years all say they want to make money, develop people, and have fun. Sadly, there is often an imbalance in favor of the first goal to the detriment of the final two. In order to achieve all three, you simply must learn and practice effective delegation skills, a major developmental strategy that ultimately achieves all three elements of success.

If you feel in your heart that developing your people is not your responsibility, then this book will be of little interest or value to you. You should discard it and read instead about stress management. However, if you feel you have the dual responsibility of generating profit through the sale of goods/services and simultaneously developing your people, then this book is going to be a fun read.

Delegation Defined

In my view, there is only one true definition of delegation: "Delegation of authority means the leader has a clear understanding with a subordinate that the subordinate has the power to make decisions and to act, within explicit limits, without checking with the leader first."[2] Delegation of authority means that the main objective of delegation is to shift decision-making authority to someone else, usually a subordinate.

When we dissect the definition of delegation, we find three essential elements. First, there is a clear assignment of duties, goals, and expectations. The driving force behind these inputs is clear communication. The delegator must decide exactly what needs to happen. To help bring clarity to this critical preparation step, write down exactly what you expect. Then effectively communicate that picture to the delegatee. Ask appropriate questions to be absolutely sure the delegatee has the same picture in mind. The discussion constitutes the validation phase after which the delegatee knows he/she knows.

The meeting concludes with the confirmation phase, which lets the delegatee know that you know he/she knows. For example, in a coaching session several years ago, my client was the typical Type A who chafed at what he considered a waste of his valuable time. "I work with intelligent people. I don't think it is really necessary to waste time on 'validation' and 'confirmation,'" he said.

Later that day, while observing his delegation interview, I tactfully encouraged him to "finish the job." In doing so, he learned two valuable lessons.

First, although he thought he had clearly explained his objectives, limitations and expectations to the employee, he learned such was not the case at all. Some of the terms he had used had a somewhat different meaning to the delegatee. This uncertainty reduced her confidence and increased stress.

Second, in the confirmation phase, when the delegatee stated correctly, in her own words, exactly the duties, goals, and expectations, both parties gained two important intangibles: enthusiasm and ownership on the part of the delegatee plus confidence and trust in the mind of the boss. Invariably, such important mutual feelings are always reflected in nonverbal communication and true bonding occurs.

"Yep," my client said sheepishly, "if I had not finished the job with the validation and confirmation phases, we both would have devoted much more time sorting out the train wreck."

The second clause in the definition of delegation implies the granting and accepting of the authority inherent in the task. If the task is to open an office in a designated city, the delegatee must have written authority, in advance, to hire staff, lease real estate, contract for utilities, etc.

The third element is the creation of commitment, i.e., the moral compulsion to perform. When people fully understand their duties, goals, and expectations, and they have the required authority to accomplish their tasks, they tend to be committed.

Notice I said "tend to be" committed. There is no guarantee they will be, but I can guarantee they will not be committed if they don't clearly understand the task and/or do not have the authority to accomplish it.

How can you tell if people are committed? While they do not wear "I am committed" or "I could not care less" sandwich signs, their level of commitment can almost be that obvious if you observe carefully. Those people who are neither committed to the company nor to the customer are easy to spot. They come to work reluctantly and go home enthusiastically. They are experts at what they *don't* have to do; they stop working at the last period in their job descriptions.

Where people are uncommitted, the parking lot is an unsafe place at quitting time. They are not "going home." They are "leaving work"! These sad souls find no joy or pleasure at work. They work to earn enough money to help find fulfillment off the job in hobbies, sports, church, and civic activities.

Organizations composed of uncommitted people reek of mediocrity, conflict, and stress, and no one has any fun. Customers who observe such behavior will lose confidence in the company, as well as its products and services, and soon will "fire the company" and do business with a competitor.

However, when people are totally committed to the company, the customer, and more importantly, to each other, they come to work enthusiastically and go home reluctantly. They are not concerned about quitting time. Their job descriptions are viewed as a loosely phrased framework of opportunities to "wow" the customer daily. They find joy, challenge, fulfillment, and yes, even fun, on the job. They leave work so energized that they often make significant leadership contributions off the job in recreational, religious, and civic activities.

Can you imagine what your customers might think by observing such behavior from your employees, both on and off the job? In our free enterprise system, success is usually driven by the sales process. All sales start with a positive response to these two questions:

1. *Do I have confidence in this person?*

2. *Do I have confidence in the company/organization this person represents?*

If the prospective customer answers no to either or both of these questions, there will be no sale. Bottom line: delegation creates commitment, commitment creates confidence, and confidence creates sales, which support the bottom line. It's that simple.

Three 'Ts'

The crown jewel, delegation, stands on a three-legged pedestal: **time, training, and trust**. Farmers use a three-legged stool to milk their cows in the barn. Just as a three-legged stool is stable on any terrain, even on an uneven barn floor (a four-legged stool requires a flat surface for stability), so it is with the three *Ts* of delegation.

The first *T* means there simply must be an up-front investment of *time* in order to put all the puzzle pieces in place. I once heard the major difference between a politician and a statesman—a politician is concerned about the next election (short-term), and a statesman is concerned about the next generation (long-term).

There is a parallel in delegation. If you are going to be a statesman in management, you need to expand your objectives to include the next generation of the company. But, rest assured, once the delegation machine is running smoothly, the invested hours are returned to you many times over.

You will learn in a later chapter that one of the most valued benefits that flow to people who delegate effectively is having much more quality time to accomplish more important tasks—tasks which return greater value to the organization than the task that was delegated. But, like any investment strategy, you must let the process mature over time to reap the full rewards.

In one client company, I met with a recently promoted manager who was completely stressed out. I asked about his major responsibilities. He blurted out, with a grin, "I am in charge of Hot Projects, Panics, and Big Deals." As we chatted, I learned that since his recent promotion, he was desperately trying to learn his new job—while continuing to do his old job and training his replacement.

It turned out that in his old job, he had rarely delegated. Sadly, he had not developed anyone to take his place. He was performing quite well on one part of his old job, juggling the one ball called "push product out the door."

However, when he was promoted unexpectedly due to his boss's resignation, our hero was faced with the overwhelming challenge of juggling three balls: (1) learn new job, (2) do old job, and (3) train replacement. He was terminated when all three balls came crashing to the floor in front of a key customer.

The bad news is that it is virtually impossible to devote quality time to delegation when you are in a constant state of crisis management. The reality is that *if you don't delegate, then you can't delegate*.

You must fully appreciate the value and necessity of slowing the train down long enough to invest high-quality time to develop your staff through delegation.

When we return to the business basics, the first objective of the enterprise is not to maximize profits—it is survival. Think of delegation as driving a piling deep into the soul of the organization. You cannot drive a piling overnight—it takes time. Yes, delegation is a *time*-sensitive strategy.

The second *T* is *training*. If the delegatee lacks any of the skills required to successfully complete the delegated task, you must provide the necessary skill-building training. Don't stop training until the delegatee has demonstrated the ability to accomplish the task to an acceptable level without close supervision. Then document that training to create accountability.

Training (skill transfer) means "to become *proficient* through *instruction* and *practice* in a climate of high self-esteem." There are a few key words in this definition: *proficient* means acquiring the ability to do a task to an acceptable level of performance.

There are four different standards that define acceptable performance: quality (error free), quantity (an adequate number), cost effectiveness (not wasting valuable resources to accomplish the task), and timeliness (due date or deadline).

Instruction and Practice. Very often the quality of learning is directly related to the quality of the teaching. Delivering good training or instruction is an art. While we cannot devote adequate attention to proper training techniques here, there are many excellent programs to address such issues.[3]

Practice is absolutely essential to skill building. Think of some skill or task that you have virtually mastered. Focusing on something you know you do very well lowers your stress. When you think of the activity at which you are proficient, your self-esteem goes up and your stress goes down, since self-esteem and stress operate inversely.

Can you recall the very first time you tried something at which you are very proficient today? Probably not. The healthy human mind tends to suppress unpleasant experiences. Did you do it correctly or did you muff it up? When your first attempt was unsuccessful, you might have responded to the embarrassing situation and thought, "I really blew that; I'm not going to do that again!"

But you didn't. You were mature enough to think instead, "What did I learn about this task that I can use next time to become better?" You recognized that the mistakes we make are usually temporary, but the lessons they teach us are permanent. You are good at certain tasks today because you learned a valuable lesson from every iteration.

I cannot count the number of times I have witnessed performance problems caused by poor training. The mere fact that the boss *showed* employees how to do a task, or *told* them how to do it, or gave them a book/manual that *explained* how to do it, does not guarantee they learned how to do it. Employees eventually must perform the task! This process of the trainee's actually accomplishing the task properly (without help) creates that important sense of closure that *lets him know that he knows*! (validation phase).

I confess to being a fanatic about the value of high-quality training. *You can never motivate an untrained person!*

Motivation (willingness) is created through the application of consequences, both positive and negative. The following *exaggerated* example makes the point that there is a huge difference between training and motivation. For more than 50 years, I have been an active pilot, with some 12,000 flying hours. My next-door neighbor, Mike, is a very intelligent and successful president of his construction company. He has told me many times that he has always wanted to learn to pilot a plane but just never had the opportunity.

Here are the facts: Mike is smart but untrained as a pilot. Let's see if I can motivate him to perform (fly my plane today) by providing overwhelming positive and negative consequences. "Mike," I say, "if you fly my plane solo today, I will give you $10,000,000 cash (highly motivational positive consequence). However, if you fail to do so, I will put you in jail for the rest of your life." Ouch! (Highly feared negative consequences for nonperformance!) Will Mike perform (fly)? Of course not! Regardless of the motivational consequences, no performance occurs, because Mike is untrained.

This is an outrageous example, but I have seen many companies lose customers and good employees shortly after implementing the cost-cutting policy of trimming the training budget to bare bones, purchasing cheap (poor) training, and then trying to motivate their employees by adding a few dollars to the incentive program and commission structure. The customer fires the company because the employees are untrained to perform to the demands/expectations of the customer. Hence, no sale and no commission—you get the picture. The only way to create skills (ability) is through effective training—there's no other way.

Now for the good news. *Good training is inherently motivational.* When people experience excellent training, they internalize (own) the valued skills, and repeatedly use and develop those skills which result in high performance. High performance builds self-esteem, reduces stress, and "wows" the customer, who then buys more products and services. Some of the most valued positive intangible consequences, which are highly motivational, are the resulting feelings of accomplishment, pride, and enhanced self-worth, plus the attendant praise and affirmation. Despite rumors to the contrary, good training is motivational, but motivational consequences never create skills.

The final *T* of the pedestal is *trust*—an elusive intangible but as real as a mother's love. How does trust develop between two people? It takes time to establish a trusting relationship. When we first meet someone, we do not openly *distrust* that person; we move to a neutral "wait and see" position. We *wait* to learn which direction the pendulum moves. The sad part is that the most innocuous, subtle behaviors, which are filtered through our own values and perceptions, influence our trust levels. When people do what they promise to do when they promise to do it, when they refuse to spread rumors and gossip, and when they make decisions based on principles rather than group norms and politics—these and myriad other factors influence whether or not we trust them.

Another important piece of this puzzle is how effectively and often we communicate that trust to others. Let's assume that my many years of working with my editor, Chapman Greer, Ph.D., has led me to believe her to be honest, sincere, and candid in our interactions. In my heart of hearts, I trust her. However, further assume that my words and actions have never communicated that feeling of trust to her. The result is that because I have failed to convey my total trust, she perceives either a lack of trust or worse yet, distrust, and thus fails to perform to capacity. The greatest benefit of genuinely communicating trust is that when trust is received and perceived, it creates confidence. Confidence's first cousin is enthusiasm. Ralph Waldo Emerson told us years ago: "Nothing of value has ever been achieved without enthusiasm." He is still right.

Unfortunately, if you trust someone and fail to communicate that trust, confidence is lost, enthusiasm fades, and the trust leg of the pedestal collapses. Which leg in a three-legged stool is most important? All of them. And so it is with delegation. All three elements—time, training, and trust—are absolutely essential to the process.

Leadership is not a label;
it's a process.

Developing trust takes time.

Punishment does not ensure
high performance; it only
ensures absence of the poor
performance that earned the
punishment. Punishment only
ensures mediocrity.

chapter TWO
The Benefits

People do things for their own reasons, not ours. Behind every action is at least one or more motivating factor. The first thing a successful salesperson learns is that people are attracted to products, not because of their features (characteristics, color, speed, etc.) but because of the benefits those features will deliver. Herein lies the major paradox of selling. Features are tangible, measurable, and objective; benefits are the output of how each person perceives the features as he filters objective data through his own set of personal values and past experiences.

Effective delegation produces a broad spectrum of benefits. In this chapter, we'll look at the benefits that flow to the person delegating, to the delegatee, and finally, to an organization and its customers when delegation occurs.

Benefits that flow to the 'delegator'

Delegation frees up time for more important (high-value) activities. As we discussed in the first chapter, you must invest quality time on the front end to successfully complete all the steps in the delegation process. Ultimately, however, the time you invest in delegation will be returned to you many times over.

You may recall in the Introduction that Joe worked 60 to 70 hours per week. After he delegated effectively, he worked only 35 to 40 hours per week and was a more effective executive. Some writers refer to this benefit as escaping the activity trap.   Joe found more time to reconnect with his wife and son and to become healthy—all important factors for success.

Delegation develops trust between the boss and subordinates. One of the three legs of delegation is trust, a fragile concept at best. Trust creates high self-esteem, reduces stress, opens communication, and helps to create confidence. I have visited ailing companies where the employees simply did not trust senior management. Delegation will help to resolve some critical trust issues.

In the mid-80s, I was consulting with a company in New England. The major malady appeared to be a lack of trust between the CEO and a Vice President. My assessment interviews revealed that the CEO was a demanding, impatient, and threatening leader. When he asked for information at staff meetings, he wanted it "now or I'll find someone else for your position who is more responsive and really on top of the job!"

Such a leadership style virtually eliminates the likelihood that any manager will ever delegate. This lack of delegation was perceived by the department heads as a lack of trust. Delegation *requires* open communication, plus the development of trust; yet neither of these elements existed.

Sadly, I was unable to convince the CEO of the value and benefits of delegation. I have always felt my failure to influence change in the situation contributed, in some way, to the firm's eventual bankruptcy.

Delegation creates better decision-makers. The boss's main activity is making decisions; if he/she is the only person able to make decisions, then every decision, no matter how trivial, will end up on the boss's desk. By delegating some of that decision-making workload to a subordinate, a senior manager can teach decision-making skills to others and fairly evaluate that process, and at the same time devote more attention to the high-impact decisions.

I am persuaded that decision making is another skill that must be learned, much like learning to ride a bicycle. Decision-making responsibilities and authority come instantly with the carpeted office and big oak desk. Unfortunately, those important decision-making *skills* are learned the old-fashioned way, through practice, practice, and more practice.

Since delegation is an adventure in decision making, for every delegated task, there is a direct benefit in decision-making practice. Great decision makers do not learn the craft by starting with major life or death decisions—they learn under the gracious guidance of a delegator who has a sincere interest in the delegatee's eventually becoming a truly great decision maker.

Delegation gives the boss more time for creativity, reflection and coaching. One of the consistent responses I have heard from executives whom I have taught to delegate is, "When I delegate, I am under less time pressure. I actually have time to think through a problem and discuss it in depth with my team. We have the quality time to devote to important decisions."

The truly effective CEOs I have known appear to be "above the fray." They are not distracted by the crisis du jour. They are focused on the long-term mission and values. Their team members invariably respond to such leadership and gain strength and confidence in the company and themselves when the CEO has time to contemplate and place today's problems in a broader mission context.

Delegation enhances the boss's promotability. When a boss who has been delegating effectively is on a short list for promotion, the choice could be influenced by the training impact on his/her department if he/she is promoted. A delegator tends to have less "turbulence" or training/replacement activity than someone who has not delegated. Most people want to move up in the organization, but promotions are usually competitive. When you delegate and create some "bench strength" from which to draw a suitable replacement, you have created for *yourself* a competitive edge for the next promotion.

Delegation increases productivity and raises morale. In most companies where productivity and morale are high, we find that quality, customer service, employee retention, and profits are high as well. And we see attendant decreases in turnover, errors, training costs, lawsuits, and conflict.

These are only a few of the various benefits that flow to managers who learn and practice effective delegation skills.

There are also many "wins" for the person to whom a task is being delegated—the delegatee.

Benefits that flow to the 'delegatee'

Since delegation requires a willing co-conspirator (delegatee), let's discuss what's in it for the person selected to receive the delegated tasks.

The delegatee learns the delegation process, which can be used in delegating tasks to subordinates. When this occurs, the delegatee now becomes a delegator and reaps all the aforementioned benefits. This cascading effect can easily move the process several levels down the organization. There is a multiplicative effect when one person delegates effectively and encourages delegatees to do likewise.

The delegatee becomes more promotable since he has learned, practiced, and demonstrated decision-making skills. As people move to higher levels of authority, they normally make more important decisions and those decisions have a greater impact on the company and the customer. Delegation can be considered a decision-making training program.

Delegation enhances the job security of the delegatee. In most large organizations where layoffs are possible, I sense there is a "hit list" tucked away in some corporate vault. This list contains the names of employees in descending order of value; the top of the list is reserved for the most valuable employee, who would never be laid off, and at the bottom of the list is the person most likely to receive the first pink slip. When a person has been selected to receive a delegated task or project, new skills tend to move him/her up the list.

In recent years, due to economic and competitive pressures, countless organizations have downsized or "right-sized." That's code for "fired many people." In discussions with senior executives about the re-engineering strategy, I gained the following insight. The first wave of downsizing is usually perceived by management, and most employees, as producing a positive effect on the company. Management has a graceful way of getting rid of the least productive and least valued employees. The only folks upset are those first few marginal employees who are asked to leave. In all candor, most everyone else is truly glad to get rid of some "dead wood."

With each successive round of layoffs, the process becomes more difficult and "gut wrenching" for the decision makers. In truth, whether a person stays or goes ultimately becomes the hard choice of determining who is of the greatest value to the company's success. The final decision often turns on which employees have limited skills, although they are competent, in contrast with those employees who have broader skill sets. In professional sports, the player who only plays one position is more likely to be let go than a solid utility player, who can perform adequately wherever and whenever needed. Therefore, delegation tends to create utility employees who are of great value.

Delegation gives the delegatee leadership clout. When a VP delegates a task or project to her department manager, allowing that person to make decisions (spend money, commit resources, assess risk, etc.), that process is observed by the department manager's employees. When the employees approach their department manager for a decision, they get one. At the second level of logic, this is what the employees soon perceive. "My department manager's boss (VP) has such confidence in my immediate boss that she is empowered to make important decisions."

The next linkage in the employee's mind is, "I also have confidence in my boss." In a word, the delegation process validates the delegatee in the eyes of their employees, which gives the delegatee "leadership clout."

Unfortunately, the converse is also true. If the VP chooses not to delegate, regardless of the reason, the would-be delegatee is seen as not being trusted by the boss. This lack of trust tends to erode a person's ability to motivate and inspire his/her own employees.

Delegation creates involvement and ownership. When people are allowed to make decisions, they tend to own the consequences for those decisions, both good and bad.

If the outcome is positive, they experience pride. Conversely, if the result is poor, they tend to accept accountability and look for solutions and lessons learned. Rarely do we see delegatees playing the "blame game" because of a poor outcome.

Benefits that flow to the organization and customer

When delegation is effective, benefits flow to the entire organization and, in turn, to its customers.

Delegation results in faster decision making. The earliest possible time a decision can be made is when the information, talent, and authority lines converge for the first time. Let's assume a customer needs a decision on a particular problem. If the salesperson has been delegated the authority to make an appropriate decision, then the customer's needs are met instantly. However, if that decision authority is restricted to a higher level of management, then the customer must wait until the appropriate decision maker can be consulted. During the "decision delay time," the customer has time to tell others how unresponsive and unimpressive your organization appears. The longer the wait, the more frustrated and vocal the customer will become.

One of the ways that retailer Nordstrom has become legendary (and extremely profitable) is the simple truth that its managers empower salespeople to make decisions that benefit the customer and delegate the authority to do so.

Managers delegate effectively and employees work to meet the customer's need immediately. In this world of instant gratification, a good or acceptable solution delivered on time from the person in the trenches is often better for all concerned than the best solution from management delivered too late.

Delegation reduces internal paperwork and its attendant costs. In organizations where delegation is scarce, most decisions are made at the upper management levels. If you look closely, you will see that many of the reports, studies, presentations, recommendations, analyses, etc. are really required to support managerial decision making. If delegation were used to push some of those decision points to lower levels, there would be less need for much of the internal paperwork.

Delegation builds teamwork and enhances morale. One can hardly escape the sense of teamwork that results when people, at various levels, are involved in the decision-making process. High morale is the by-product of many inputs—delegation is a major component of high morale.

Finally, *delegation improves performance, productivity, and profit.* I do not need to support this contention with examples or evidence. If you have been in business for 24 hours, you know this claim is true.

There are many benefits, direct and indirect, tangible and intangible, that flow to everyone involved in the delegation process. But real-world experiences reveal that many people deprive themselves of the benefits by succumbing to the power of barriers that restrict, inhibit, and discourage delegation.

Let's shine a light in those dark corners.

The mistakes we make are usually temporary, but the lessons they teach us are permanent.

Good listeners listen with their ears and eyes. They are also aware of what's not being said.

Always treat your employees like you want them to treat your most important customer— because they will.

"

If no one's following, then
you're not leading.

Lead your organization to top
performance—and have fun
doing it.

Leadership exists in the minds of
the followers.

chapter THREE
The Barriers

Managers offer all kinds of reasons for not delegating; some of which are valid. Most are just excuses and present unnecessary barriers. Let us see how these barriers are perceived by the delegator and delegatee. Finally, let's discuss barriers across the organization.

Barriers in the delegator

"I can do it better myself." I cannot count the number of times I have heard this rationalization from swamped, stressed-out executives. The *I-can-do-it-better-myself* barrier is difficult to eliminate because it is grounded in a foundation of good intentions. The manager is faced, at least in the short term, with the thorny dilemma of delegating a task to someone who is less experienced. The underlying assumption is that the subordinate's decision making and subsequent performance will be flawed when compared to the work of the more skilled boss.

You may recall our hero, Joe, in the Introduction. He sincerely wanted the best possible work from his department. His tragic flaw was that this barrier was operational in every situation when delegation was a viable option. To rationalize not delegating, managers often use the following binary logic: "Would my boss want me to knowingly produce work that does *not* reflect this department's best effort?" They answer, "Of course not!" and thus fail to delegate again. Sadly, the cycle continues to spiral into eventual disaster.

I must admit that as a consultant and coach, this is one of the most difficult barriers to neutralize. In fact, on a few occasions, I have failed to persuade, convince, or cajole my client into understanding the following deeper, long-term issues.

For example, Janet has been the department manager for five years. She is extremely capable, has a depth of experience, and is highly respected by her boss, peers, and subordinates. In a word, she is a superstar, and everyone knows it. She's been affirmed so often that she feels that she is the most capable person in the department, and she probably is.

Enter Ashley, one of Janet's strongest employees. Janet considers delegating a task to Ashley, which will require that Ashley consider alternatives, then select and implement one—decision making and action-planning in the purest form.

Janet asks Ashley for her recommendations, and Ashley replies with her best shot. While listening to Ashley's ideas, Janet reflects on the core of experience she herself gained years ago, when she made a similar decision, only to realize later the flaws in that choice. Based on that experience, Janet has already made a decision. Because Janet is the boss, she owns 51 percent of the stock in the relationship with Ashley. In a genuine effort to help Ashley, Janet says, "I understand your idea but let's do it this way."

When such words are spoken by a boss, the subordinate decodes that as "My boss has just ordered me to use her decision, and I should deposit my recommendation in the trash as I leave her office."

While it is quite possible that Janet's decision is, in fact, better, the organization gains only the marginal value difference between Janet's and Ashley's choices. Honestly, there have been many times when my subordinate's decisions were far better than mine, but many people are understandably reluctant to press the issue with their bosses.

If Janet is controlled by this subtle barrier because she's gaining the benefit of the "best" decision, how much time and effort (sweat equity) will Ashley be willing to invest in the next opportunity to make a decision? Precious little!

Let's fast forward to Act III of this tragedy. Because the *I-can-do-it-better-myself* barrier is operational, Ashley never gets the opportunity to enhance her core of experience and become a better decision-maker, as Janet did several years ago. The "Ashleys" I have met, who want to learn, grow, and develop, will not continue to sit on the bench for very long. Making decisions, implementing them, owning them, and learning from them are analogous to an athlete's getting into the game. Only those athletes with a dirty uniform at the end of the game can enjoy any sense of pride and achievement for the victory or feel a sense of loss for the defeat.

The saddest part of the scenario is that Ashley, the potentially high performer, will soon respond to calls from headhunters and be snatched away by a competitor. Recent research reveals that the true cost of personnel turnover is one and a half times the departee's annual salary! Too high? Not when you consider the cost of the training that Ashley will take with her when she leaves, as well as the cost of recruiting, interviewing, and testing all the candidates to select another "Ashley." And don't forget the cost to train the new employee and allow time for him/her to become a productive member of the corporate team.

It is all but impossible to convince well-meaning people like Janet that the desire to select and implement the absolutely best decision may, in reality, purge the company of the next generation of managerial talent, costing the company money and helping to reduce the training budget of your competitors.

In most decision-making situations, there is usually a *range* of acceptable alternatives, as opposed to just one choice, i.e., the boss' solution. On a scale of 1 to 10 (in which 10 is best) Janet's decision is, in fact, a 10. As she listens to Ashley's choice, Janet will degrade Ashley's choice against her 10 standard. Let's further assume that Janet rates Ashley's decision an 8. Janet focuses on the difference of "2" as she discards Ashley's 8 in favor of her 10.

However, if Janet has defined a range of acceptable decisions, say 6 to 10, then, any decision above 6 is acceptable. When viewed in this broader context, Ashley's

8 is a fully acceptable, albeit not the best, option. If Janet thinks beyond the *I-can-do-it-better-myself* barrier, she will allow Ashley to implement her decision.

Now, Janet will lose the 2-point better decision, but what will she gain? Brace yourself! She will gain Ashley's involvement, commitment, and enthusiasm, which comes from Ashley's getting off the bench. It's fair to project that Ashley will invest a lot more "sweat equity" in the next decision; that's how she learns to make choices that are 9s.

Please note that I am not suggesting the boss accept unacceptable decisions, e.g., 5s, when 6s are the minimum. Nor am I recommending that the boss *always* implement the subordinate's acceptable option; sometimes the boss will choose her/her own ideas. The benefit of this random strategy is that since Ashley never knows when her ideas will be accepted and implemented, she will always be prepared.

When people prepare thoroughly to offer alternatives to their bosses, they develop better skills and insights in decision making. The Ashleys of the world read this process as "development," and they love it!

In summary, there are valid reasons for a boss to occasionally accept the barrier that *I-can-do-it-better-myself,* but if used to excess, there are huge losses for everyone involved. I have found this barrier to be one of the most pervasive and difficult to neutralize because it's based on the best intentions.

Another common barrier is the fact that the boss *simply does not know how to delegate properly.* In countless interviews I have asked managers, "Do you delegate to your staff?" A consistent reply is, "Whenever I try to delegate, my people often drop the ball or screw up the project; I spend a lot of my valuable time in damage control."

If I ask how they actually delegate a task, most say they bring the employee into the office and tell the employee what task is to be done. They stress that if the employee has problems, the door is always open. While this typical remark sounds acceptable to the uninitiated, as you read through this book and actually learn how to delegate effectively, you will realize that many well-meaning managers may *think* they know how to delegate, but sadly, don't have a clue.

The first problem to be solved in performance management or delegation is "lack of skill or knowledge."

The main purpose of this book is to destroy the barrier of inability, i.e., to teach managers precisely how to delegate effectively without losing control.

High-control needs represent a barrier that restricts or inhibits delegation. There are several causes of this problem. First, the boss may, in fact, be required to have immediate recall of details, which can only be known by the one who has personally accomplished a task. Delegation would require the boss to conduct research and gather facts in order to reply to a request or an update from his own supervisor. If this time delay or lack of on-the-spot knowledge would be viewed negatively by his own supervisor, then rest assured, the boss will not put himself at risk by delegating.

On the other hand, this need for tight control may exist only in the imagination of the potential delegator and may not be required by his own supervisor at all. This barrier is insidious because the manager often does not realize that his dilemma is self-imposed.

When I was a lieutenant colonel and Air Force detachment commander, I worked with Don, a young captain and an Air Force Academy graduate. One day I asked Don for some information and said I needed it by close of business the following day. Immediately he stood up smartly and began to spout facts and figures to three decimal places. When he concluded his recitation, he stood there, fully expecting me to congratulate him for his immediate control of the minutia. The next few minutes were a bit unpleasant for Don.

While I was impressed that he had devoted all that time to capturing, updating, and memorizing those facts, he was paid too much by the Air Force to waste his time and attention on such matters. He had a secretary and support people who were paid to have the information available for him, and for me, when we needed it to make decisions.

This was not an emergency situation; close of business tomorrow was well within decision time. I wanted Don, as an Air Force captain, to have his mind, heart, and enthusiasm engaged in more important issues that challenged an officer of his considerable talent and intellect. I didn't want him wasting the taxpayers' money by majoring in minors! He told me years later, "That chat we had really helped me focus on the *important few* over the *trivial many*." Don learned to delegate; that skill served him well as he was promoted to higher levels of command.

Another barrier which discourages delegation is good, old-fashioned *insecurity*. This does not normally surface in the early stages of my coaching interviews, but subtle probing usually reveals this bit of fluff. In a typical interview, I ask what other risks the client sees that would cause him/her to defer delegation to another day.

I am often asked, "If the staff is making all the great decisions, and getting the credit, why does my boss need me?" Managers often feel they were promoted to their positions because they were able to make sound business decisions. And they feel obligated in their new position to make even more, not fewer, decisions.

Dealing with this barrier requires a paradigm shift along the lines of the truism: "Give a man a fish, and you feed him for a day. Teach him how to fish, and you feed him for a lifetime." Managers need to understand that they are not out of the decision-making business but have expanded into the development business as well.

Because they are delegating effectively, without losing control, they are reaping all the many benefits to themselves, their subordinates, the company, and the customer. In other words, they will not only feel positively about the decisions they make, but more importantly, about the manifold benefits of delegating and developing the next generation of managers. The manager who is delegating should be honored for these and other positive results of delegating.

A final barrier that creeps into the picture is the seductive *self-esteem* one gets from making decisions for subordinates and taking the credit, both publicly and psychologically. Often, the motivating factor is insecurity from such thoughts as "If I delegate decision making to my staff, that will make me less valuable."

For example, the door opens to Mary's office. Julie asks her boss, "What should I do about the Wilson account?" Mary ponders the situation for two nanoseconds and issues an excellent answer (decision). Julie jots down the decision, nods respectfully, and departs to apply her boss's decision to the Wilson account. Mary looks out the window and mutters under her breath, "Damn, I'm good." That night, over dinner, she remarks proudly to her spouse, "I had a very productive day. I am proud of the decisions I made for my staff."

As Mary matures as a manager and becomes comfortable with delegation, a valuable skill in her managerial tool bag, the dinner conversation sounds more like this: "I had a wonderful day at the office. I made five decisions for my staff, but Bill, Harry, Julie, and Sue each made several excellent decisions today. They are really growing in their jobs and are enthusiastic about their accounts. I am really proud of how they have developed their decision-making skills."

Several months later Mary arrives home, on time, kisses her husband, and says enthusiastically, "I had an absolutely fantastic day at the office. My staff is hitting home runs with their accounts. I didn't have to make a single decision today. Not one! Let's go out for dinner!" That former monster/barrier of *insecurity* whimpers off as Mary says to herself, "Damn, I'm good!"

Barriers in the subordinate

Why would anyone who has the benefits of delegation close at hand refuse to participate as a delegatee or receiver? There are several barriers that cause otherwise positive people to choose the negative road.

The first barrier the prospective delegatee may use is the old, *"it's not my job"* trick. Yes, it's not your job. Jobs are just an array of tasks. People don't do jobs—they do tasks. We need to help the delegatee appreciate the fact that the boss is merely delegating one task to him, which only adds one more task to his current task list. He is not doing the boss's job—he is only doing one of the boss's tasks.

When a person offers this objection, the delegator has failed to "sell the task" to the delegatee. Selling involves stacking sufficient positive consequences (benefits) for the delegatee, which creates willingness.

A case in point, Mark was recently transferred into Jill's department. Over the next month, Jill tells her new employee that she understood he had some experience in budget preparation in his previous position. When she was in the position he now holds in this department, the previous department head who was promoted to VP got Jill involved in the department budget preparation and presentation. Jill feels the opportunity to present the budget to the senior executives taught her a lot about the company, and she gained positive visibility with the senior staff. She feels it had a big influence on her promotion to department head.

In a few months, Jill would like Mark to assist her with the budget preparation and presentation. She plans to delegate that task to Mark in a few months if he is interested.

If Mark has a modicum of street smarts and ambition, he will reply enthusiastically, "Sure, Jill. I look forward to the opportunity." Nowhere in that exchange will Mark ever think or say—*it's not my job*, because Jill has stacked the benefits so high that the *it's-not-my-job* barrier has been buried.

Other barriers relate to the four broad categories of poor or nonperformance. *Lack of skill or knowledge* must be addressed first. The skills must be in place before anything good can happen. Any skilled delegator will ensure that the delegatee has the ability to perform the assigned task properly. (We will deal with the skill issue thoroughly in Chapter 5 in our delegation interview.) After we have assured that the skills are in place, we will shift our attention to resources.

Task interference poses another potential barrier for the delegatee. Lacking the necessary resources (tools, equipment, money, time, people, support, etc.), a person will surely fail, due to task interference. The delegation interview will, of course, deal with this issue, as well.

A final barrier is the possibility of the *appearance of favoritism*. Negative peer pressure is a real demotivator if the delegatee senses her co-workers will think she is trying to earn points with the boss. This problem can be countered if the boss has an established policy and, more importantly, a practice of not singling out one person for development. Everyone should have an equal opportunity to learn and grow through the delegation process.

While you would think most people would jump at the opportunity to become a delegatee and inherit all the related benefits, as we have shown, there are several barriers that can prevent the benefits from flowing. Now, let's see what barriers lurk within the halls of organizations.

Barriers in the organization

After we have neutralized or destroyed the barriers for the supervisor and the subordinate, we must finally handle a few negative factors in the organization that would limit the opportunity or interest in delegation.

Show me an organization with *no value for training and development*, and I will show you an organization where people do not delegate. Since learning to delegate properly involves training dollars, the math is simple—no value (dollars) for training equals no delegation skills.

Another problem I have encountered is what we call the one-man—or one-woman-show policy. Imagine a person who has been a senior manager for many years, who also has high control needs. That person feels he/she is the only person who can make proper decisions. Therefore, every decision, no matter how trivial, is made by that person—and that person only. This soon strangles every ounce of interest, ownership, and commitment from everyone in the organization. High turnover invariably follows.

Finally, zero tolerance for mistakes discourages people from delegating. If those who delegate are routinely reprimanded or disciplined for minor errors made by their delegatees, the delegators learn very quickly that the risks outweigh the benefits. When a well-meaning perfectionist punishes delegators for minor errors by delegatees, she actually strangles the life out of the delegation process. I know only two solutions for this destructive behavior. First, fire the "strangler" or second, coach her until there is full understanding of the delegation process. Studying this book would be a good start.

In conclusion, there are many barriers that can deprive the delegator, the delegatee, the organization, and, in turn, the customer of the incredible benefits of delegation. As we proceed, please notice how the steps in the delegation process virtually destroy each and every barrier.

Even lousy employees expect good leadership.

Sharing your knowledge and skills with your subordinates does not diminish you as a person.

People learn more, learn faster, and make fewer mistakes when their self-esteem is high.

chapter FOUR
The Preparation

Selecting a task to delegate

The benefits of delegation abound, but only if we proceed with the process and actually delegate a task. How do we determine which of our many decision-making tasks are suitable to delegate?

Permit me to use a football analogy to help identify a task. The quarterback has the option of handing the football to a running back or passing the ball to a receiver who is running downfield in hopes of catching the pass. Think of the football as the task that is to be transferred from one player to another. Although there is only one football, there are dozens of tasks from which to choose.

To choose a task, review all the various tasks you accomplish to see if one recurs in a relatively short window of time. You may have been preparing a monthly report for the past several years. With such *recurring tasks*, you have gained experience; you know what works and what doesn't. If you establish some reasonable standards or limits, you may be able to delegate this task to a subordinate. Let's assume you have discretion to make adjustments for any problem not exceeding $5,000; your zone of decision-making authority ranges from $1 to $5,000. However, with proper training, a delegatee can be given authority to resolve all problems not exceeding $3,000; his zone of authority ranges from $1 to $3,000; yours is now $3,001 to $5,000.

A second group of tasks to delegate should be those that *require too much of your time*. When you calculate your hourly salary, then calculate the hours you consume on the task, you may learn that the resulting value of the task to the organization is less than the money you are paid for doing it. Consider delegating that task to someone at a lower pay grade; this may bring the cost/benefit ratio into balance.

Other suitable tasks to delegate are those important, high-visibility *developmental tasks*—you don't just "pass the trash." In one client-company, being selected to be on the budget preparation/presentation team was a king/queen-maker task. Historically, people who were delegated such tasks gained valuable high-level visibility. Promotions were not far behind.

Later in the practice exercise, in Chapter 5, you will need to select a real task to delegate; I suggest you choose one now from the above categories of suitable tasks. Once you have chosen a task to delegate, ask yourself the following questions:

1. *Do I have proper authority to delegate this task?* There may be some legal or regulatory restrictions on delegating this task. For example, federal banking restrictions may state that no person below the vice-president level may sign a particular document. Therefore, the task of signing that document could not be delegated. A personal example comes from my role as the commander of an Air Force base. One of the commander's responsibilities is to *personally* authorize all searches and seizures on the base.

Security Police officers and their K-9 drug dogs pass realistic training exercises to verify that there is valid probable cause to search a vehicle or home for drugs. Both the commander and the deputy base commander are also certified so they can authorize searches.

Because federal law states that "the base commander will personally authorize searches," when I went on vacation, orders were published relieving me of command for that week and designating the deputy as the commander. This task could not be delegated to someone holding the position of deputy. If you find there are restrictions on delegating a task, you have two options. First, don't delegate it, or second, request permission from the appropriate authority for a waiver to the restriction or regulation.

2. *Does delegating this task involve decision making?* Since delegating is primarily the shifting of decision-making authority, if no decisions are involved, then you are not delegating. You are merely assigning additional staff work.

3. *Will delegating this task develop the employee and build morale?* If the employee has never performed this task, then delegating it to him can both develop the employee's professional skills and build his morale as a result of the accomplishment.

However, there are occasions when delegating a task will not build morale. If you are faced with an unpleasant task, such as disciplining or terminating an employee, your delegating this particular task may leave the impression with your employees that you lack character and courage. If this happens, respect and morale plummet. I am sure you can use these litmus test questions to ensure you are on firm ground when you select a task to delegate.

To whom should you delegate?

Permit me to continue to use the football analogy to explain the process of selecting the most suitable candidate to become your delegatee—the person to whom you will delegate a task. In football, the quarterback is the field general and makes scores of decisions during a game. Let's think of the delegator (boss) as the quarterback in an organization. When a quarterback calls a pass play, he takes the ball from the center, steps back into a pocket provided by his defensive linemen, and must make a multi-variable decision in three to four seconds: Which receiver is in the best position to catch the pass and make a touchdown?

If we transfer this situation to an organization, we can appreciate that a boss must conduct a similar assessment to choose the best possible delegatee, with the highest probability of successfully accomplishing the delegated task.

These are the specific decision variables the boss must consider in selecting the best possible candidate. We are assuming you have already developed a short list of hot prospects; here's how you select the winner:

1. *Which candidate has the requisite skills and knowledge to accomplish the task properly?* A review of training records, performance reports, and your personal knowledge will help narrow the field. The better-trained candidate requires less additional training. If training (skill transfer) is needed, use appropriate training techniques to ensure the candidate can demonstrate the ability to accomplish the task properly. Document the training to establish accountability. During the delegation interview, one step is devoted to asking questions to ensure the necessary skills are in place.

2. *Which candidate already has all or most of the required resources—tools, equipment, time, etc.?* If any resources are absent, take direct and indirect action to prevent task interference problems.

3. *Which candidate appears to have the highest level of motivation (willingness)?* During the delegation interview, ask questions to learn if the consequence system (benefits) is in balance in the mind of the

chosen candidate. Take action to ensure that valued, positive consequences follow good performance. Promise only what you can personally deliver. Make every effort to set the consequences in the candidate's personal value system. For example, a single mother with small children will not value the consequence of "more overnight travel." An unmarried man or woman may enjoy that consequence, while the single mom might enjoy more flextime.

An adequate analysis of these three questions with respect to each candidate will help the boss (quarterback) to select the best possible delegatee (receiver) to properly accomplish the task.

Touchdown!

78

The three most important factors that determine the success of any human endeavor—leadership, leadership, leadership.

We tend to get what we reinforce and honor.

You can either choose to be a boss and get employees who work for their paycheck, or you can choose to be a coach and get team players who work for the customer. Pick one.

"

There are more than a thousand ways to motivate people; money is only one.

Truly great leaders are equally effective in a wide variety of situations.

When you are listening, two good things are happening: first, you are stroking the other person, and second, you are learning.

chapter FIVE
The Delegation Process

In my first book, *Managing to Get the Job Done*,[4] we shared the four broad categories of poor/impaired performance.

1. *Lack of skill/knowledge:* The most cost-effective and valued training is to "train against the deficit." There's little return in teaching people skills they already possess or skills they don't need. All training should begin with a needs or gap analysis. When delegating, we must ensure that the delegator has the skills to delegate effectively without losing control, *and* that the delegatee has the skills to perform the delegated task properly.

2. *Imbalance of consequences:* Both the delegator and the delegatee must perceive sufficient highly valued positive consequences (benefits) to create the motivation (willingness) to participate in the delegation process. Chapter 2 lists several benefits that flow to the boss, the employee and the company/customer when effective delegation

occurs. Remember, when listing benefits resulting from delegation, resist the temptation to tell the employee of benefits that flow to you, the boss (i.e. . . will reduce my work load. . . will take some pressure off me). Newsflash! Most employees care little about benefits that flow to their boss. Be sure to stack benefits that are of interest and value to the employee.

3. *Task interference problems* result when employees do not have the required resources (tools, equipment, information, people, space, time, etc.) to perform the task. Both the delegator and delegatee must possess the resources to succeed in their respective roles.

4. *Lack of feedback or poor feedback:* In order to ensure success for both parties, there must be a feedback system in place with controls and realtime corrective action.

As you study the following delegation interview guide, you will notice that all of these critical performance problems are solved.

Delegation Interview Guide

In Appendix II, you will find a form to use in actually delegating a task. What follows is a discussion of what each letter in the acrostic D-E-L-E-G-A-T-E stands for so you can prepare for that all-important, one-on-one delegation interview.

D—*Describe* the task and expected results.

Jot down succinctly what you want the person to accomplish and set general expectations. The four lines are designed to limit your notes; do not go into too much detail at this stage. For example, "I would like you to prepare the monthly vehicle utilization report."

E—*Explain* the purpose.

List here the reasons this task must be accomplished. For example, "The vehicle utilization report is required by Department of Transportation regulations and the Internal Revenue Service." When the purpose is explained, it tends to enhance motivation (willingness) because the subordinate will appreciate the fact that the vehicle utilization report is "very important." We are not yet focusing on the benefits that flow to all involved, but only on the overarching purpose.

L—*List* the benefits that flow to the delegatee, the organization, and/or the customer.

Caution: There is a great temptation to list benefits that accrue to you, the boss. ("Your doing this task will save me time.") Benefits (positive consequences) that flow to you don't do squat for your subordinate's motivation. Review Chapter 2 and list some of the benefits that are enjoyed by the subordinate and/or the organization, and ultimately, the customer.

E—*Examine* the skills and abilities.

If you have not personally witnessed or do not have firsthand knowledge that the subordinate possesses all the discrete skills to accomplish the task successfully, then you must ask focused questions to determine the skill level. Avoid the tempting "bad" questions: "You can do this task, can't you?" Subordinates can respond "yes" because they can do it, "yes" because they think they can but really can't, or "yes" because they know they can't but are too embarrassed or too intimidated to admit the truth. That's three "yes" answers and you still do not really know if the skills are actually in place.

It is far wiser to avoid questions that draw upon subjective feelings and opinions. Good questions include, "When was the last time you accomplished a similar task?" "What was the result or outcome?" "Have you had any difficulty recently in accomplishing a task requiring similar skills?" In other words, ask questions that remove all reasonable doubt about the actual level of skills. If additional skill transfer (training) is indicated, then take the appropriate action and record the training to establish accountability.

G—*Give* authority formally, and set explicit limits.

One of the most powerful statements of trust, which builds confidence, is to formally convey decision-making authority to another person. When you tell that person (verbally, or better yet, in writing) and their colleagues as well, "You have the decision-making authority to spend up to $10,000, hire up to four people at this particular pay grade, and make certain exceptions to policy within specific limits," you are, in fact, delegating. Delegation is basically a shift in certain decision-making authority to a lower level.

In Chapter 1, the definition of delegation says "Delegation of authority means that the leader has a clear understanding with a subordinate that the subordinate has the power to make decisions *and to act, within explicit limits, without checking with the leader first.*" Now we need to set the limits within which the decision-making authority can be exercised:

- *Time limits.* "By the second business day, each month, before 5:00 p.m."

- *Resource limits.* "You can only spend $1,000 and may only hire two temporary employees at pay grade level one."

- *Space (geographical) limits.* "Do not go beyond the county line, or district area."

- *Explicit limits that remove uncertainty and reduce stress.* "Do not offer refunds unless the customer is on our 'A' list of major customers."

At this point in the delegation interview, the delegatee should have a crystal-clear picture of the task, the purpose, the benefits, the skills, and exactly what his/her authority covers and what it does not.

A—*Assign* resources.

Determine all the resources (tools, manuals, equipment, time, people, authorizations, etc.) the delegatee will need in order to prevent task interference. Assign all the needed resources up front. Don't hassle the person by doling these out one at a time.

There is a very subtle potential problem in this step. Let's assume you have delegated a task to someone on your staff and some of the inputs (resources) come from others on your staff. When *you* were accomplishing this task, your request for inputs was grounded in your position power with respect to your staff. They were predisposed to send their boss the required inputs on time and of excellent quality.

However, now one of their co-workers, the delegatee, will be asking for the inputs that were previously sent to you. The bad news is that some co-workers, particularly those that may be senior in longevity and/or position, may not respond as promptly to that same request. The input request may not be as high on your employees' "worry list" as it once was. There is the potential for the delegatee to suffer task interference problems due to the lack of timely input.

The best way to prevent this unpleasant situation is what I call "down-field blocking." You, the boss, must inform everyone on your staff that a request from the delegatee for inputs is done "in my name; I am confident you will support the delegatee as effectively as you have supported me in the past."

T—*Teach* and establish the control process.

You will recall that the fourth broad category of poor/impaired performance was "lack of feedback or poor feedback." The feedback step is basically the control system. Any and all effective control systems must have four major elements.

First, you must have a *quantifiable and measurable goal or standard*. That's why the limits must be explicit. Let's assume you must manage (or control) $100,000 during one calendar year. The ideal standard of control is to manage the expenditure of those limited funds in order to accomplish your mission, avoid crisis management, and in the best of all worlds, spend the last dollar on the last day. No, we're not dreaming; a proper control system can produce such results.

Second, you must have a *monitoring system that tracks performance* in exactly the same terms as the goal or standard is expressed. If your goal is in dollars per year, then track dollars per year. If the goal is in man-hours, then track man-hours.

Third, you must have a *realtime system of comparing where you are at a particular point in time with where you should be if you were in perfect control.* For example, if you are programmed to spend 25 percent of your money by the end of the first quarter and you have actually spent 25 percent, then you are in perfect control. But it's an imperfect world; so what if you have spent 35 percent of your funds by the end of the first quarter? Do you have a problem? Not necessarily. Figure 1 in Appendix I will explain why.

The fourth and final element of a control system is *corrective action.* Before you begin the project, you choose several corrective actions to be implemented if you are not in control at a given point in time. For example, if you spend 30 percent of your funds in the first quarter, you have prearranged to reduce overtime, lay off temporary employees, or implement appropriate cost-cutting measures.

These corrective actions are developed, coordinated, and approved *before* you are actually in an out-of-control condition so that these corrective action decisions will be made with ample time to think through them. If we wait until the operation is already out of control, there tends to be panic, time pressure, and emotion—three bad ingredients for making sound decisions. Furthermore, if everyone knows in advance what will happen if the situation gets out of control (work weekends and nights), there is a subtle motivation to monitor closely and stay on track. (Please see Appendix I for a detailed discussion of the control process.)

E—*Express* your appreciation to the delegatee in advance for the fine job you are confident he or she will do.

This final step brings a sense of closure. Remember, people learn more, learn faster, and make fewer mistakes when their self-esteem is high. Undertaking any new task will always create some nervousness and stress. The last thing the delegatee hears when leaving your office is, "Thank you for accepting this important task/project/assignment. I am looking forward to our first control meeting on (date) at (time)."

When this process is followed to the letter, most delegatees will approach the project with enthusiasm and confidence. You will recall in Chapter 1, "Delegation Defined," we stressed the importance of validation and confirmation. The process described above ensures that the four major performance problems are solved:

1. Lack of skill/knowledge (ability)

2. Imbalance of consequences (motivation)

3. Task interference (resources)

4. Lack of feedback/poor feedback (control)

However, this recipe for delegation, when followed precisely, also ensures that two critical elements—validation and confirmation—are in place for both the delegator and delegatee.

"

Your boss doesn't promote
or fire you—your people do.

If you can't measure it, then
you can't celebrate achieving it.

It's not what leaders know that
matters; it's what they do.

"

Your people can make your work
either a joy or a living hell;
fortunately, you decide how
well you lead them.

"The most important single
ingredient in the formula of
success is knowing how to get
along with people."

Theodore Roosevelt

Do not stumble over things behind
you.

chapter SIX
Post-Delegation Problems

Delegation can be a fragile strategy. I want to expose and destroy four problems that can harm this valuable process even after you have delegated perfectly.

First, *don't take the project back at the first sign of trouble.* If you have disciplined yourself to wait until the first control meeting to meet with the delegatee (see Appendix I), then you won't be tempted to intervene prematurely. However, if at the first control meeting you find that the project is not exactly where it should be, there is a strong tug at your "psyche" to say, "Things are not going too well; I'll take over from here." Big mistake!

Instead, examine the current performance to determine if it is within the control zone. If so, you simply take the planned corrective action and work toward the next milestone. If the two of you have designed the control system properly, it is virtually impossible to exceed the control zone, especially when the early phase of the control zone is so broad. However, if your delegatee has gone over the control zone fence, then more drastic actions are warranted, but still resist the temptation to "take it back." The major downside of succumbing to this temptation is that you lose confidence in the delegatee, he loses confidence in you and in himself, and even worse, everyone loses confidence in the delegation process.

A second potential problem is *holding on to the project by failing to delegate all the required authority, resources, and support at the outset.* Don't create a situation in which the delegatee is required to constantly return to you for the next bit of authority. This act of asking "Mother, may I?" is demeaning, inefficient, and time consuming for both of you. Delegate the complete package, set limits and schedules, then get out of the delegatee's way.

Third, *do not undercut the delegatee by encouraging or allowing the delegatee's subordinate to come to you for decisions.* There are two faces to this flaw: 1. If the boss makes a decision concerning a project/task that has been delegated to a subordinate, this tends to overrule the subordinate. 2. It also undercuts the subordinate in the eyes of his employees. This is similar to the *I-can-do-it-better-myself* barrier in the boss, but this problem occurs *after* the fact.

No good can come from teaching employees that a decision can be made by two people. If they don't like or agree with the decision of the delegatee, they may ask you, the delegator, for a different decision. Rest assured, some employees will test the waters in this game. If they come to you for a decision your delegatee is charged to make, I strongly suggest you send them packing with such terse words as, "I have delegated that decision to your boss, and I support his/her decision. I am disappointed that you would even consider asking me to make that decision. Good day." When the delegatee's employees experience that message in your office, they will never come back for a second helping. Ultimately you, the delegatee, and the employees, all will win. Never undercut or overrule those to whom you have delegated responsibilities.

Finally, *do not hover.* I once had a client who had delegated a very important task to a competent woman who was willing and able to do a great job. However, her boss was so uptight and nervous, he all but moved his desk into her office! He asked for updates, status, problems, and concerns, almost every day. Not only does such behavior take valuable time from both parties, but it also virtually screams to the delegatee and to everyone else—I DON'T TRUST YOU! The inevitable consequence of this message is that the trust "leg of the pedestal" collapses; the delegatee loses confidence and quite likely fails. If you delegate properly and establish effective controls, you will not be tempted to hover. President Theodore Roosevelt said: "The best executive is the one who has sense enough to pick good people to do what he wants done, and self-restraint enough to keep from meddling with them while they do it."

Before we close I want to share one more lesson I learned the hard way from a salty old Air Force colonel when I was a lieutenant in Germany in 1962. As the base training officer, I was responsible for ensuring that 4,000 military and civilian personnel had completed their annual training requirements. I was in the headquarters and worked closely with the unit-level training officers in the 20 units assigned to the base.

I routinely scheduled one meeting a week with my boss, the colonel. One day, I was briefing him on more bad news than good news. He interrupted, "Pete, I have enough problems of my own; I don't need yours. What you have done is put your problems on my desk." He reached in his center desk drawer and produced a five-by-seven-inch laminated card on which was written in bold type—"DBMP-BMA" and handed it to me. "What do you think those letters stand for?" he asked. After a moment of reflection I mumbled, "Don't bring me problems—bring me answers."

"Right," he replied. "As an officer responsible for the base training program, your job is to think of answers, develop solutions, and get results."

I sheepishly assessed my briefing notes to find he was correct. I had very few solutions or recommendations to offer my boss; I had been guilty of thinking like a follower (tell me what to do) and not like a leader (here's what I am going to do). I returned the card, tucked my tail between my legs, and slithered out under the closed door. In spite of the professional embarrassment, that was an important developmental moment for me; I thanked the colonel later for a valuable lesson. In my years as a manager, I have given the DBMP-BMA card to a few young executives. They too have thanked me later.

What I have described is "reverse delegation." As a manager, be sure your staff does not develop the subtle art of delegating their problems upward to you.

"

If the only solution you have is a "hammer," then all problems look like a "nail."

Technical skills are as different from management skills as success is from failure.

You cannot motivate an untrained person to perform.

"

Hearing is a mechanical
process; listening is a skill that
takes practice and effort to master.

Everybody wants to win.

The number-one goal of any
business organization is survival.

epilogue

In April 1971 I was sent to Vietnam as an Air Force major to fly combat missions over the Ho Chi Minh Trail in Laos. En route to Southeast Asia, all pilots were required to attend a two-week jungle survival school at Clark Air Base in the Philippines. The purpose of the school was to teach the skills needed to live in the jungle, evade capture, and escape if we were ever shot down.

On the first morning of the course, an extremely impressive survival instructor opened the session with the following words: "Gentlemen, a few months ago, a pilot, just like you, sat in this class, just like you. On his twenty-second mission he was shot down, and he ejected over Laos. Three days later he was successfully rescued. When the doctors examined him, they found he was in excellent health and had gained a few pounds. You see, that pilot bailed out and landed in a 'grocery store.' He paid attention in this class, read the assignments, and knew where to find gallons of pure water and plenty of nourishing food. He knew how to conceal himself from the enemy and how to signal for help;

he had learned all the skills we taught him and he not only survived but also thrived."

My instructor continued, "Sadly, there was another pilot, just like you, in that same class. But he decided to party at night and sleep through class; he was too busy playing to read the homework assignments. He too was shot down and landed in the same jungle. After seven days of overlapping mistakes, some of which put him and the rescue helicopter crews in peril, he was finally rescued. When the doctors examined him, they found he was dehydrated, starving, and disoriented. Today, as you start this course, you get to decide if you want to land in a grocery store or a jungle." That was one of the most effective motivational moments of my life. Rest assured, no one in my class slept through the course.

So how does that story relate to you, a manager? Believe me, learning how to delegate effectively without losing control is an executive survival skill. By learning and applying the concepts and skills in business, you will not only survive, you will thrive—because it's a jungle out there!

" Customers really don't care if the hands that serve them are male or female, black or white, young or old. They only want those hands to be skilled and willing to serve.

Almost everyone is selling something. Even my preacher says he sells "fire insurance.

"

Learning is fun; learning more is
more fun.

Happiness is a healthy organization.

Loyalty, creativity, and
commitment are never for sale;
you have to earn them through
strong leadership.

"

appendix I

Control Process

The most basic control chart is in Figure 1 (on the next page).

To demonstrate the value of an effective, realtime control system, let's assume that you want to manage (control) your $100,000 budget during the fiscal year. For tracking purposes, we will divide the year into four quarters. If it were a perfect world, we would spend the last dollar on December 31, without the excitement of crisis management. But, regrettably, perfection is rare. So let's learn techniques to reduce some of the inevitable risk the future holds. I suggest the following steps:

Step 1: Determine the planning parameters, e.g., "What we are going to spend money on this year?" Review the line items in the previous budget and update/revise as needed.

Step 2: Involve the most knowledgeable people available in estimating how much money you expect to spend on each line item in the first quarter. Add all the

108

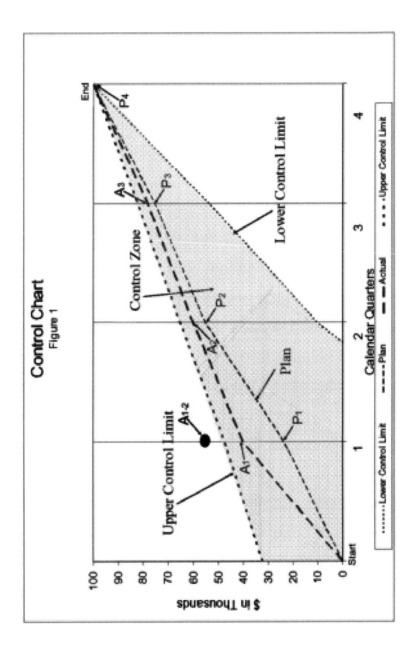

estimates and plot the total at point P1. This is your planned expenditures at the end of the first quarter.

Step 3: Repeat this process for the remaining three quarters and plot P2, P3, and P4. By connecting these projections, you have plotted your plan. You can select any date and determine the level of your planned expenditures for that date.

Step 4: Using the collective best judgment of your group, create a lower control limit. Since on January 1, you have 12 months and $100,000 of latitude, the beginning portion of the lower control limit can be very wide. However, as the year progresses, you have less time and less money available, so the control limits will neck down to zero variance (same as the plan) on December 31.

Step 5: Repeat the process to establish an upper control limit; it will also neck down to zero variance on December 31. The shaded area is the "control zone," as defined by the upper and lower control limits.

These five steps are completed before the year begins. The major advantage of establishing a reasonable control zone is that, since you can consider any plot of actual performance that falls *within* it, you will not be in a crisis situation. Take pre-planned normal corrective action to respond to those factors which cause the deviation, and target the second-quarter projection, P2.

If, however, actual performance data fall outside the control zone, significant corrective action is appropriate. Fortunately, if you control the operation as I suggest, it is highly unlikely that you will be faced with a crisis. Sound impossible? It's not, if you closely follow the procedures I will share.

During your delegation interview, you will reach the step identified by the letter T; it stands for *teach and establish the control process*. If the delegatee is not familiar with the control process, then you must teach him/her the process, using this book. Your purpose is to bring the delegatee to a level of understanding so that he/she can actively participate in creating the control system for the project. You, the delegator, and your subordinate, the delegatee, should mutually develop every aspect of the control system, e.g., jointly develop the list of planning parameters, etc.

What should be the most logical window of time between control meetings? What should be the upper and lower control limits? What will "in control" look like at each milestone? What is your corrective action going to be for each possible out-of-control situation? In a word, you facilitate a discussion that results in the delegatee's creating (and owning) the control system.

After all the preliminary planning is completed, you let the delegatee proceed with the project. That's why the last step in the delegation interview is E, express appreciation and confidence.

The first control meeting or milestone in the example at Figure 1 is April 1, one day after the end of the first quarter.

After totaling all the expenditures for the first quarter, you find that instead of spending $2,000 as planned, the delegatee has actually spent $3,500—point A1—$1,500 more than planned. Do we have a crisis? No. We are still well within the control zone; hence, we are concerned, but we are not in a real crisis. Had we spent $5,500 in the first quarter, A1-2, we would be beyond the upper control limit and, therefore, out of control. Now you have a *genuine* crisis.

We are lucky that the control zone at the first milestone is quite large, because we have three more quarters and lots of money remaining. Our ultimate goal is to spend the last dollar on the last day, P4, without experiencing a crisis.

When you draw the dashed line from the starting point to A1, you will notice that the slope of the planned line and the actual line is different. The next step not only provides insight but is also an excellent opportunity for coaching:

The three classic coaching questions, in order, include:

1. **What did you do _well_ in this activity?** (or in this example, in the last quarter?) This allows the delegatee to recount the positive activities he was aware of consciously. Be sure to encourage that person to write down the positive activities. After they have finished, you, the coach, can relate the positive activities that were not mentioned; these items were unconscious. Your sharing these now brings them to the conscious level and also should be written down.

2. **If you could do this activity (last 90 days) over again, what would you do _differently_, if anything?** This gives the employee an opportunity to be self-critical. This environment tends to be less threatening and creates more openness to an honest self-evaluation, which surfaces areas of improvement. The employee will, no doubt, cite a few situations he/she could have handled better. People do not

become defensive and argumentative with self-criticism. After they have recalled, and recorded, those activities that offer opportunities for improvement, you may want to tactfully ask questions to draw attention to a few "subconscious" opportunities.

Resist the temptation to ask accusatory questions like, "Why did you do that?" or "What went wrong with that activity?" Such questions often result in defensiveness and argument.

I suggest questions like, "Would you help me understand your thinking behind that activity?" Or "What do you think caused that situation to occur?"

Record the responses.

3. **What did you _learn_ this past quarter about how to successfully conduct this activity?** This third and final question always results in a review of the positive and negative lessons learned, plus this often reveals some insight or revelation not directly discussed previously. Be sure the delegatee personally records the lessons and insights learned. Armed with these valuable coaching lessons, he/she dives headlong into the next quarter with the

confidence that comes from success and effective coaching.

The slope analysis is accomplished by a simple comparison of the projected expenditure for each planning parameter with the actual expenditure for that parameter (e.g. P1 vs. A1; P2 vs. A2). If you planned to spend $680 on fuel but actually spent $750, the difference explains, in part, the reason the slopes were different. You may find additional variance or offsetting variances.

After this analysis, you will learn what the major causal factors were. This information will lead to a reasonable and effective corrective action. Implement that action and target your expenses toward point P2 at the end of the second quarter. As you begin the second quarter, you will have gained valuable insight into your operation and how to keep it on track.

At the end of the second quarter, you find the actual expense plots at A2, which is slightly above the planned goal of P2. Repeat the analysis process and coaching. However, this time, you are drawing upon the learning curve gained in the first two quarters. Implement the planned midyear corrective action and target point P3. Please notice that the control zone is becoming narrower, since we have less time and less money remaining.

The good news is that you are much smarter and know your operation far better in the final stages because of the slope analysis corrective action and coaching at each milestone.

At A3, continue this process of perform, plot, analyze, coach, and correct; then proceed toward point P4, your final objective from the outset.

I have seen companies with huge budgets use this disciplined process and literally spend the last dollar on the last day—with less stress and more fun.

appendix II

Delegation Interview Guide

Use this guide to conduct the interview in which the formal delegation process begins. Permission is granted to reproduce this interview guide for your personal use. It is not to be duplicated or sold without written permission from Peter A. Land. See page 122 for contact information.

Subordinate ————————————————————

Date of Interview ————————————————

D - Describe the task and expected results. ——————

————————————————————————————

————————————————————————————

————————————————————————————

E - Explain the purpose. ——————————————

————————————————————————————

————————————————————————————

————————————————————————————

L - List the benefits to the organization and employee.

————————————————————————————

————————————————————————————

————————————————————————————

E - Examine the skills and ability. ————————————

———————————————————————

———————————————————————

———————————————————————

———————————————————————

G - Give the authority formally and set limits. ——————

———————————————————————

———————————————————————

———————————————————————

A - Assign the resources ——————————————

———————————————————————

———————————————————————

———————————————————————

T - Teach and establish the control process. ——————

———————————————————————

———————————————————————

———————————————————————

1.   Determine the planning parameters and standards.

———————————————————————

———————————————————————

_____

_____

2.   Determine the tracking system. (Get the subordinate to help determine the tracking system.) ————————

_____

_____

_____

3.   Determine what "in control" looks like at a given point in time. (How and when will this take place?) ————————

_____

_____

_____

4.   Take corrective action. (Discuss possible corrective actions.) ————————————————————————

_____

_____

_____

_____

E - Express your appreciation and confidence. Schedule and confirm first control meeting. ─────────────────────

───

───

endnotes

1 Dale D. McConkey, *No-Nonsense Delegation* (New York: AMACOM, 1974).

2 John Douglass and Joseph F. Massie, *Managing: A Contemporary Introduction* (Englewood Cliffs, N.J.; Prentice-Hall, Inc. 1973), 107.

3 Ken Blanchard Companies, www.kenblanchard.com

4 Peter A. Land, *Managing to Get the Job Done* (High Point, N.C.; Executive Press, 1998).

order information

Additional copies of *How to Delegate Effectively without Losing Control* may be purchased for $15.95 per copy plus $3.00 for shipping and handling. Send check or money order to the following address:

Peter A. Land Associates, Inc.

4210 Lomac Street

Montgomery, AL 36106

Please allow three to four weeks for processing and delivery.

Call our office to inquire about prices for quantity discounts: **334-271-2639**.

For additional information about Pete Land, his other publications, or his speaking and training engagements, visit our website: **www.peteland.com**.

Notes